Go Ho... ...!

Thea Franklin

Illustrated by Olga & Aleksey Ivanov

Rigby®

A Harcourt Achieve Imprint

www.Rigby.com
1-800-531-5015

"Is my mother here?"
said Chick.

"Go home, Chick!"
said Duck.

"Is my mother here?"
said Chick.

"Go home, Chick!"
said Cow.

"Is my mother here?"
said Chick.

"Go home, Chick!"
said Horse.

"Is my mother here?"
said Chick.

"Go home, Chick!"
said Rabbit.

"Is my mother here?"
said Chick.

"Go home, Chick!"
said Pig.

"Is my mother here?"
said Chick.

"Go home, Chick!"
said Dog.

"Is my mother here?"
said Chick.

"Welcome home,
Chick!" said Mother.